A Simple Guide

to

Golf

by

Russ Jarvis

LUMINIS BOOKS
Published by Luminis Books
1950 East Greyhound Pass, #18, PMB 280
Carmel, Indiana, 46033, U.S.A.

PUBLISHER'S NOTICE

The Publisher and Author make no warranties or representations regarding the accuracy or completeness of this work and disclaim all warranties, including without limitation warranties of fitness for a particular purpose. The information contained in this guide may not be suitable for every situation, and the Publisher is not engaged in providing legal, accounting, or other professional services. Some information and links on the Internet change frequently. The Publisher is not responsible for content on third party websites referenced in this work and does not endorse any organization or information provided on such sites. Neither the Publisher nor Author shall be liable for damages arising herefrom.

Cover art direction and design by Luminis Books. Cover photo courtesy of Shutterstock.

ISBN-10: 1-935462-65-2
ISBN-13: 978-1-935462-65-1
Printed in the United States of America

10 9 8 7 6 5 4 3 2 1

Simple Guides

give you

Just the Facts

Get up to speed with golf—fast!

Simple Guides: get you started quickly.

No extra clutter, no extra reading.

Learn all of the specialized lingo of golf, what **equipment to use,** as well as all the essential golf etiquette **you need to play an enjoyable round.**

Learn about the lofty world of **professional golf, including all the major tournaments.**

Have fun learning about all kinds of specialized golf games, and find out everything you need to **play a round of golf and start having fun!**

To John Tefft – my uncle who introduced me to a lifetime of enjoyment on the fairways

About the Author

Russ Jarvis started playing golf at age ten. It took him another 17 years to begin a serious writing life. Since then, he has published two novels, and his numerous articles have appeared in various magazines, journals, and newspapers. After 24 years in parish ministry, he now works in the field of professional healthcare chaplaincy. *A Simple Guide to Golf* is his first non-fiction book. He lives in Central Indiana with his wife Nadine, where they enjoy four grown children, five grandchildren, and a new stray cat named Camo.

Table of Contents

Introduction

You probably picked up this little book for one of two reasons:

- You love golf, or
- Someone you care about loves golf

According to a 2009 study by the National Golf Foundation, 28.6 million people above the age of six claimed to play golf that year in the United States alone.[1] 25% of that total are women. Multiply that by the average household size of 2.59 and you have a total of 59,207,000 Americans who either play golf or are in a meaningful relationship with someone who wants to know why golf matters to them so much. This is almost 20% of the total US population! Add the figure of those who don't play, but who admit to watching professional golf on television from the January tournaments in Hawaii all the way to the December shootouts in Florida, and the total of golf-oriented persons climbs even higher.

Those who are passionate about golf wonder why everyone else isn't.

An excerpt from another golfing writer says it well:

"Though I have played many other games and even been a bit fanatical about some of them, golf holds a special place in my heart. I love to play the game, to watch it played by others (especially those better than I am), and to read about its history and traditions. Those who have never played the game might

---

[1] Golflink.com

find it difficult to understand or to appreciate the passion that golf can inspire in people who do play, but everyone who has played for any length of time has experienced that feeling. There simply is no other game like it."[2]

On the other hand, those who don't play wonder why anyone would. This book can help remove the wedge of misunderstanding that often comes between golfers and those who love them.

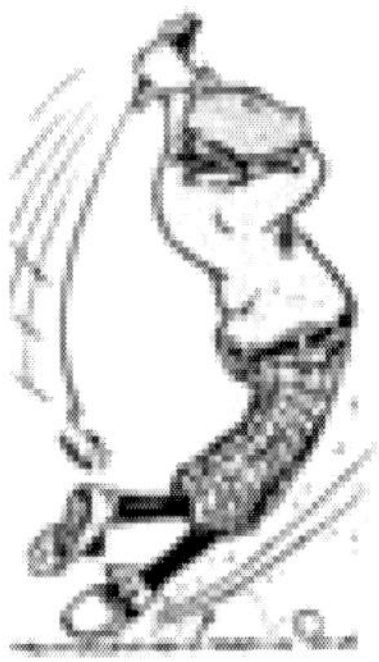

What you won't find in this book:

- Instructions on how to play like a pro. (I've never broken 80.)
- Boring statistics such as "percentage of greens in regulation (GIR)."
- Pedestrian tributes to famous players either ancient or modern.
- Much space given to the Rules of Golf as determined by the Royal and Ancient Golf Club of St. Andrews, Scotland (a 162 page volume with a twenty-three page index).
- Hopefully anything considered sleep-inducing by non-golfers.

What you will find in this book:

- A brief history of a centuries-old game that endures in popularity.

[2] Mike Linder, *Play it as It Lies*, p. 1.

- Understanding of terms like "driver" and "iron," and why a golfer might shout "be right!" after he hits a ball, but would never shout "be left!"
- Advice on how to behave properly on a golf course so that your playing partners and the authorities ("The Marshall") allow you to return.
- An orientation to the current American golf tours. (This is important because golfers like to imagine themselves enjoying the lifestyle and skills of their professional brothers and sisters.)
- Basic instructions on the ways golf is played in the United States.
- And—most importantly — help to share the passion of that special person who may often leave you puzzled over his or her pursuit of "pars" and "birdies."

Among the many things golfers say is "Golf is a lot like life." While this little book may not lower your handicap, it could boost your relationship score.

Chapter 1

A Brief History of an Ancient Game

When Did Humans Start Playing Golf?

Golf's origins are much debated. It seems that various cultures have entertained themselves with games that resembled modern golf.

February in the Netherlands typically brings periods of slushy snow and temperatures close to freezing.[3] Nevertheless, on February 26, 1297, someone in a village along the Vecht River wrote a record of his neighbors playing a game that consisted of hitting a leather ball with a stick. The winner was whoever used the least number of strokes to hit the ball into a target several hundred yards away.

- The French played a game called *chambot*. An early British sport was *cambuca*, meaning "hooked rod or stick" referring to the implement used to play the game.
- A tapestry dating from the Ming dynasty (CE 1368 – 1644) shows a member of the Chinese court engaged in *chuiwan*, a

[3] Lonely Planet.com

game already centuries old at the time where one swings a club at a small ball with the aim of sinking it into a hole.

- First century Roman legionnaires followed up their triumphal parades with a game called *paganica* that called for hitting a stuffed leather ball with a bent stick.
- Hundreds of years earlier, the Persians played a golf-like game known as *chaugán* when they weren't trying to figure out how to defeat Alexander the Great's army.

Early Golf

The game that is played today around the world has its roots in Scotland – interestingly enough, another climate known for slushy snows and freezing temperatures.

The word "golf" (Scottish *gouf*) is thought to be an alteration of the Dutch *colf* meaning "stick," "club," or "bat." The first documented mention of golf in Scotland appears in a 1457 Act of the Scottish Parliament. It seems that King James II of Scotland had grown nervous regarding his homeland security. He wanted a more effective fighting force. So he banned golf as an "unprofitable sport" and decided that his men should focus on archery. He failed to understand how deadly golf balls could be to bystanders when struck by strong, but poorly-skilled persons. This may reveal the roots of the term "golf hacker."

Golf courses did not start out having eighteen holes. In the fifteenth century, a course at St. Andrews, Scotland featured eleven holes, laid out end to end from the clubhouse to the far end of the property. Golfers played the holes outward, then turned around and played the holes in reverse for a total of twenty-two holes. It must have been a time when golfers were in great shape. Think about it. After the eleventh hole, you had to retrace your steps to find the tee again, play the hole, and then backtrack to the previous hole's next tee which was a fairway away. Just thinking about it is tiring!

Few things change more slowly than a golf club's constitution. After a mere three hundred years, the boomers (defined in Chapter Two) of their time decided that several of the holes at St. Andrews were too short to be challenging. They decided to combine some thereby reducing the number to nine. This made an inward and outward round of eighteen holes.

It probably surprises no one that a lawyer was the first documented person to play what we recognize as modern golf. The date was March 2, 1672. He was also a member of the House of Lords, which meant he had both the time and the means to indulge in this pastime. His course of choice – Musselburgh Links, East Lothian – is certified as the oldest in the world by Guinness World Records.

Eventually golfing societies or "clubs" formed.

- In 1744, a group of Edinburgh golfers formed *The Honourable Company of Edinburgh Golfers*.
- The *Society of St Andrews Golfers* became *The Royal and Ancient Golf Club of St. Andrews* in 1834.

- Three decades later, Scottish golfers turned their friendly matches into fierce competitions. The world's oldest continually contested golf tournament is The Open Championship, played first on October 17, 1860 at the Prestwick Golf Club, in Ayrshire, Scotland.

Golf Goes Global

The first golf club in the Western Hemisphere was the Royal Montreal (Canada) Club, formed in 1873. The game seems to have been played informally in America as far back as the 1600s, but it took until 1888 for organized golf to take hold in the United States. A Scotsman, John Reid, built a three-hole course near his home in Yonkers, New York. By the turn of the century, more than a thousand golf clubs had opened across North America.

The game of golf remained relatively unchanged - with the exception of equipment and technology – through the 20th century and into the 21st. What did change was the professional aspect of the game. Originally, the distinction between amateur and professional golfers had less to do with skill than with social class. In eighteenth and nineteenth century Britain, golf was the exclusive domain of the wealthy. Early professionals were working class men who made a living from the game in a variety of ways: caddying, greenskeeping, club making, and playing challenge matches. When golf established itself in America at the end of the 19th century it was an elite sport there as well. Early American golf clubs had to import their professionals from Britain. It was not possible to make a living solely from playing tournament golf until the mid-1900s. An American named Walter Hagen is considered to have been the first golfer to have accomplished this feat.

With the recent proliferation of professional golf tours and an entire network dedicated to the sport [NBC/ Golf Channel], it may be surprising to know that in the early days, professional golfers were disdained. Professional golfers were viewed as not much different than professional gamblers. Greater honor was given to those who played golf excellently, but as amateurs. In 1916, the Professional Golf Association of America (PGA) was founded to standardize practices and organize events. By the year 1944, twenty-two events were held. A competition between America and Britain called the Ryder Cup took place for the first time in 1927. Augusta (GA) National Golf Club was established in 1933, where the first US Masters was played in 1934. More information regarding the current professional tours can be found in chapter five.

The Evolution of Golf Equipment

Golf Clubs

Most early club makers honed their skills producing bows and arrows and other implements of war. The first recorded club maker was a gentleman named William Mayne who was appointed in 1603 to the court of England's King James I to make clubs.

Early clubs featured carved wooden heads of beech, holly, dogwood, pear, or apple. These were spliced into shafts of ash or hazel to give the club more whip or torque. Eventually, the head was improved by filling its back with lead and putting an insert of leather, horn, or bone into the club face. Skilled blacksmiths found extra income by forging iron faced clubs – initially without grooves – to provide more loft for shorter shots.

Modern club making moved away from wooden clubs with forged irons, to steel shafts, and finally to all manner of metal heads with many types of synthetic shafts. Every golfer knows that the best deals on equipment can be found in northern states at the end of golf season (October-November) when stores are clearing out their leftover supply and players are convinced that the latest driver is the answer to their troubles on the course.

Golf Balls

The earliest golf balls were wooden. In the 17th century, someone invented a hand-stitched leather ball stuffed with boiled feathers. In dry weather, a well-struck feather ball could travel 180 yards but when wet only about 150 yards. This about half the distance of the longest drives on tour these days. These featherie balls remained the only option until the mid-1800s.

In 1848, a golfing minister - another occupation noted throughout history for finding time on a golf course – named Adam Paterson, received a gift from India that was packed within a substance called gutta-percha. He discovered that the material could be softened with heat and then molded into a hard ball. This new ball was called a *gutty*. It had a smooth surface and tended to fly erratically. Players soon discovered that its performance improved after the ball received some nicks and scratches. This led to the practice of scoring newly molded balls with a hammer. The days of the feathery were over.

The gutta-percha ball lasted for approximately fifty-five years until 1903 when an American dentist named Haskell experimented with wrapping a liquid filled rubber core with strips of elastic and then covering it with a gutta-percha casing. North American golfers began to take the new ball seriously when a golfer won the 1901 United States Amateur Championship playing the Haskell ball. When another golfer used it to win the 1902 British Open Championship, golfers everywhere dropped the gutty and clamored for the new ball.

Modern golf balls are covered with more durable balata or surlyn and are made by various large corporate entities. Impress your friends by mentioning that balata is a non-elastic rubber drawn from the South American tree Manilkara bidentata. Surlyn came along because "hackers" (golfers that tend to lose and deform a lot of balls) needed a less expensive ball that stood up to their often highly damaging impacts.

More information about desirable golf equipment is found in chapter three.

Chapter 2

Golf Lingo: A Family-Friendly Non-Exhaustive List

Equipment

Bag – the container a golfer uses to hold his/her clubs, usually made of fabric or leather.

Ball Marker—a small object such as a coin used to mark the position of the ball on the green while it is lifted.

Club – a generic term describing what a golfer uses to strike a golf ball.

Club Head – the end of the club that strikes the ball.

Driver—the number 1 and largest wood. Normally the first club used on a hole other than a par three.

Grip – a rubber, leather or cloth cover that wraps around the shaft of a club so that a player is better able to hold onto it. Also the method in which one holds the club.

Iron—a club whose head is typically constructed of steel although the shaft can be of another substance. Typical lofts are between 16° and 65° and the clubs are numbed 1 through a 9 and include all wedges.

Loft - the degree of angle between the club face and the shaft. The higher the loft, the higher the ball's trajectory in flight.

Pill - the golf ball.

Putter - the club used to propel the ball across the green. It has a very flat face with no loft.

Shaft—the long straight part of a golf club. The grip covers one end while the opposite end the shaft is inserted into the clubhead.

Spikes - metal points extending from the sole of a golf shoe intended to prove additional traction when swinging a golf club. 'Soft Spikes' are made of plastic and leave less severe marks on the green. Most courses now require soft spikes and will not permit any other type.

Tee—the short straight device on which a golf ball is placed prior to hitting the first shot on any given hole. Made of wood or plastic and available in many different sizes, lengths, and colors.

Wedge—(aka: "pitching wedge", "sand wedge", "lob wedge", "third wedge", "utility wedge") The shortest club in a player's bag other than the putter. An iron with greater than 48 degrees loft. Used to play short distance shots.

Wood - the clubs normally used to hit the ball the farthest distance. Modern woods are made out of metal.

Golf Course Geography

Apron—(aka: collar or fringe) the short grass that separates the putting green from rough or fairway. Usually between 2-3 feet wide.

Back Nine/Backside — the last nine holes of an 18-hole golf course.

Bunker—any hazard on the golf course consisting of a depressed area normally filled with sand. Often found near a putting green or around the landing area of the fairway. Also called sand trap or beach.

Clubhouse - the building at a golf course that houses various aspects of the golf business including a snack bar/restaurant, locker rooms for men and women, and the pro shop.

Cup—the hole in which the flag rests. By rule, 4¼ inches in diameter.

Dogleg—any golf hole designed with a significant turn of the fairway to the right or left. Derived from the similar shape of a dog's rear leg.

Fairway—The closely cut grassy area between the tee and the green, exclusive of the rough, the green, the tee, and the hazards.

Flagstick—the long flexible pin inserted into the hole on each green with a flag attached. The purpose is so that the location of the hole can be seen from a great distance.

Front Nine/Frontside - the first nine holes of an 18-hole golf course.

Gallery - a group of spectators on a golf course, especially those who follow a golfer as he/she plays in a tournament. Casual golfers often imagine a gallery watching them as they line up putts.

Green—one of eighteen closely mown areas grass in which a hole is cut and where putting is the acceptable stroke.

Hazard—any area of a golf course designed to increase the score of a player who hits a ball into it. Most hazards contain either water or sand and are marked with red stakes or a line painted on the ground.

Hole - one of eighteen units of play within a full round of golf. Composed of a tee, fairway, and a green.

OB—out of bounds. Usually marked with white stakes or as noted on the scorecard. A ball is unplayable when hit out of bounds, regardless of whether or not it can be found.

Outside the Ropes - referring to the area on a golf course where spectators can watch tournament play. Contrasted with "inside the ropes" where the players compete.

Practice/Putting Green—a green on which players are permitted to practice their putting (and sometimes chipping). Usually located near the clubhouse.

Practice Range—a large area designated for golfers to practice various shots. When located away from a golf course it is called a Driving Range.

Pro Shop - where golfers pay green fees, purchase any needed equipment, arrange for lessons, and swap lies about how well or poorly they have been playing.

Rough—grass that is cut at a higher length than that on the fairway, tees, and greens. Players try to avoid hitting into the rough, but normally fail to do so.

Tee Box - the place where the first shot of each hole is taken. Each tee box has a number of different colors that signify different levels of play/distances to the green.

Yardage—the measurement of the length of a hole, typically stated in yards.

Score Keeping

Ace - see "Hole in One."

Albatross—a score on a hole of three (3) less than par on a par five hole. Also known as a "double eagle."

Birdie—a score of one (1) less than par for any hole.

Bogey/Bogie — a score of one (1) more than par for any hole.

Cut/Cut Line — the maximum score under which a player must score in order to be allowed to play in the next round of a tournament.

Double Bogey—a score of two (2) more than par on any hole.

Eagle—a score of two (2) less than par on any hole except a par three hole.

Even Par - any time during a round of golf that a player's score adds up to the same as par.

Handicap—the difference between the difficulty ratings of a particular course and a player's average score. This is used to allow a fair competition between golfers of different skill levels.

Hole in One—a score of one (1) on any hole. Also known as an ace.

Over Par - completing a hole of group of holes in more strokes than indicated by the established par. This is bad.

Par—the number of strokes in which a golfer is expected to complete a hole. Also, the number of strokes in which golfers are expected to complete a number of holes. Holes normally have a par score between 3-5. Eighteen-hole courses have a par between 70 and 72.

Penalty - a stroke or strokes added to a player's score due to an infraction of the rules, a ball hit out of bounds or lost, or having to move one's ball out of an unplayable location.

Stroke - an intentional swing with a club at a golf ball. The swing is added to the player's score whether he/she makes contact with the ball or not (see "Whiff")

Under Par—completing a hole or group of holes in fewer strokes than indicated by the established par. This is good.

Unplayable Lie - whenever a ball comes to rest in a location deemed not to be reasonably playable (against a rock, under a tree, etc.) According to the rules of golf the player can move the ball to a playable spot incurring a one-stroke penalty.

Whiff - when a golfer swings intentionally at a golf ball but misses it completely. Usually the occasion for a joke or rude comment by a playing partner.

Playing the Game

Address—the position of the player and the club as he/she stands over the ball preparing to take a shot.

Approach Shot—a shot taken from the fairway with the intention of reaching and staying on the green.

Away—the player in a group whose ball lies farthest from the hole. This player becomes the next to strike his ball.

Ball Mark—the indentation a ball leaves when it lands on a green. This mark is typically repaired unless the player is a self-centered and thoughtless moron.

Boomer - refers to someone who can hit a golf ball a long distance, especially from off the tee. Some boomers hit drives routinely over 350 yards. Some claim to hear sonic booms after they strike the ball but the research to prove it remains lacking.

Chip—a shot that is intended to fly for a very short distance and then roll or bounce the majority of its way towards the intended target. The intention is to stop the ball close to or in the hole.

Chunk—to hit the ball improperly by impacting the ground in front of the ball, resulting in a large divot and a shot that travels a much shorter distance than intended.

Downhill Lie—when the position of the ball is on the down slope of a hill relative to the direction of the intended target. The tendency is to launch the shot lower into the air than normal - whatever normal is.

Drive—a shot played off of a tee. The first shot on a given hole. Distance is the main objective.

Drop—the action of dropping the ball from shoulder height with an extended arm such that the ball, when it comes to a rest, is back in play. A drop is required under specific situations covered by the Rules of Golf such as recovering from an unplayable lie.

Flop Shot—a relatively short shot that travels very high and lands very softly with little or no role. Phil Mickleson is known for this kind of shot, but no one would ever call him a "flopper."

Foursome—a golfing group of four players.

In—the last nine holes of an eighteen-hole round. Derived from old Scottish links style courses where the first nine holes took players "out" from the clubhouse and the last nine holes brought them back 'in'.

Lag—a long putt that is not expected to be holed. Its purpose is to finish near the hole so as to enable a second putt that is much easier that the first.

Lay Up—a shot that is purposefully hit short of a hazard requiring another shot to circumvent the hazard. Often a player will lay up rather than 'go for it' when a steam or other water hazard crosses in front of the green. Example: "I can't get on that green in two, so I will lay up in front of the bunkers."

Lie—a term used to refer to the location and quality of the spot where a ball comes to rest following a shot. Can also be used when one golfer cannot believe that another golfer has found the ball he saw go into the woods.

Relief - allowing the relocation of a ball from a present location into a new location as dictated by the rules. A penalty stroke(s) may or may not apply.

Putt—a shot taken on a green with a putter.

Sidehill Lie - when the golfer stands below or above the ball. This often results in a shot pulled to the left or pushed to the right (for a right-handed player).

Tee Off—the act of taking the first shot on any hole, particularly the first hole of a round.

Tee Shot—the shot resulting from striking the ball off of the teeing area. The first shot of any golf hole.

Up and Down -hitting a ball in a hazard but then playing well enough to score par on the hole.

Uphill Lie - when the position of the ball is on the up slope of a hill relative to the direction of the intended target. The tendency is to launch the shot higher into the air than normal.

Path of the Ball

Backspin—the action of the ball spinning in the reverse direction to its flight. Backspin causes a ball to slow down much faster and sometimes roll backward.

Break—the curve in the path of a chip or putt to the left or right as a ball rolls over the undulations of a green. Also what a golfer might yell after experiencing some bad luck (i.e. "Give me a break!")

Carry—the distance a ball must travel in the air in order to clear an obstacle or reach an intended point.

Cut Shot—a shot that curves gradually through the air from left to right for a right handed golfer or vice-versa for a left-handed player. Usually performed to get around an intervening obstacle such as a tree.

Divot—the portion of turf ripped out of the ground by the head of the club during a swing. Also describes the patch of bare ground left after a portion of turf is torn out of the ground. Courteous players always repair their divots.

Draw—a shot that curves gently through the air from right to left for a right-handed player and vice-versa for a left-handed player.

Fade—a shot that curves or moves gently from right to left for a right handed golfer and vice-versa for a left-handed player. A very aggressive or uncontrolled fade may be termed a slice. The opposite of a draw.

Hook—a more violent, dramatic, and even uncontrollable version of a draw.

Lip Out—a putt that runs along the lip of the hole without dropping in. Typically the ball will change direction fairly dramatically. There is no such thing as a "nice" lip out.

Pin High—a shot that comes to rest roughly parallel to the flagstick, though some distance to the left or right.

Pitch—a shot that is intended to travel a relatively short distance, land softly on the green, and roll a short distance. A longer shot than a chip with a similar trajectory.

Pull—a shot that travels left to the intended line for a right-handed golfer or to the right for a left handed golfer

Push—a shot that travels right of the intended line for a right-handed golfer or to the left for a left handed golfer.

Shank—to unintentionally hit the ball directly to the side. Usually the result of striking the ball with the toe or heel of the club.

Skull—the action of hitting the ball with the leading edge or flange of an iron. The result is that the ball flies with lower trajectory and goes farther than intended.

Sky—to hit a ball extremely high in the air. This is usually unintentional and often happens on a drive when the ball is teed up too high, allowing the top of the clubhead to make contact with the ball causing it to pop up.

Slice—a shot that travels from left to right for the right-handed golfer or vice versa for a left-handed golfer. This travels at a more dramatic pace than a fade. Usually an unintentional, it is a very common shot by beginning golfers.

Wormburner—a shot with such a low trajectory that it skims the ground in a way that would appear to burn any worms crawling on the surface of the ground. Another very common shot by beginning golfers.

Things Heard During Play

Be Right - what a golfer might say to the ball in hopes of it landing near the target.

Bite - when a golfer says to a ball in hopes that it will stop quickly or, preferably, back up when it lands on the green.

Caddy/Caddie – an assistant to the golfer who is in charge of carrying the players equipment and providing advice on club selection and course layout. Most casual golfers can't afford caddies, except for willing girl or boyfriends.

Choke—describes a lack of performance in a situation where there is significant pressure for a positive outcome. Rarely used to describe one's own poor play.

On the Dance Floor - to describe a shot when the ball reaches the green and remains there. The next shot will be a putt.

Feel/Touch – having good judgment or sensitivity for golf shots.

Fore - a universal warning to other players when the flight of a struck ball puts them in danger of injury.

Gimmie—a short putt that the other player or players in a group agree would certainly be holed and therefore do not require the player to putt out (but do count one more on the score card). This is never allowed during a serious competition (except during match play when one player can "concede" an opponent's putt).

Greens Fee—the money paid to a golf course to play a round of golf.

Hacker—a golfer of very low skill who scores poorly and likely takes many divots. A golfer who has little control over his/her shots. Also called a "duffer."

Honor—the player who has the right to go first on any particular tee. This right is earned by having the lowest score on the preceding hole.

In Play—anytime the golf ball is considered 'live' or 'playable'. The ball is always "in play" unless it has gone out of play (i.e. out of bounds, lost).

Mulligan - when a golfer takes a second shot without counting the first stroke (i.e. "a do over"). This is allowed only in casual play and is a violation of golf etiquette unless his or her playing partners agree to it.

Nineteenth Hole—the bar or lounge at the clubhouse. Usually where a golfers congregate for drinks and to share stories (i.e. lies and excuses) after playing.

PGA—acronym for the Professional Golfers' Association. This organization is responsible for promoting golf and ensuring the integrity of its members regarding their ability and knowledge.

Play Through - a term used to describe a golfer or a group of golfers who pass another group on the golf course. This usually occurs because the group in front plays more slowly than the group or individual behind.

Round—eighteen holes of golf.

Sit/Sit Down - what a golfer might say to a ball in flight if it appears that the shot is going to travel past the intended target.

Short Game—the aspect of golf that is played near or on the green consisting of pitching, chipping, sand play, and putting. This is where the majority of golf shots are taken and about which most golfers spend the least time practicing.

Top - one of the most prevalent and frustrating mis-hits made by inexperienced golfers. To strike the top half of the ball with the club, normally resulting in the ball traveling directly to the ground after contact and traveling a relatively short distance.

USGA—acronym for the United States Golf Association.

Waggle—the movement of a player and his golf club at the address position. A waggle involves the back and forth movement of the club head in an attempt to get comfortable or stay loose prior to a shot.

Yips - the real or imaginary nervous twitching of muscles during a short putt that causes the ball to roll off line and not drop into the hole. The careers of many professional golfers have ended due to a "terminal case of the yips."

Chapter 3

Golf Gear: Essential and Non-Essential

My favorite Uncle John (I had three uncles who bore that first name) gave me my first set of clubs when I was twelve years old, in payment for cleaning out his garage. The putter had a wooden shaft and the irons had shafts of some kind of fiberglass. The driver and fairway wood were swiftly falling apart, the string binding unraveling from where the heads attached to their fiberglass shafts. Now I am fifty-four and I wish I had that set so I could sell it to a collector – that and the drawer full of comic books my Mom tossed out during one of our moves.

The first club I bought with my own money was a beat up 5-iron from a sale barrel at a driving range. It was my first steel-shafted club and I played with it for years until my uncle offered me an upgrade through cleaning out another of his garages.

Having purchased a new set of Haig-Ultras®, I inherited his experienced set of Wilsons®. I thought I'd gone to golf heaven. I played with that set through high school (making the team my senior year) and college (we were too small to have a team).

Since then, I have owned other sets of clubs. Recently, a neighbor helped me build my present set of irons.

Do you see a pattern here? Golfers are constantly on the lookout for a better score by means of better clubs and the golf equipment makers are pleased to provide it. A set of custom-built clubs can cost as much as $2,000. Most non-professional golfers cannot afford that price tag. Incidentally, professional golfers seldom have to buy their equipment. Golf manufacturers (Titleist®, Callaway®, Ping®, Nike®, etc.) keep them supplied with everything they need as long as they get their endorsement.

This is why your golfing loved one scopes out the weekly sale ads and websites for good deals on what he or she believes will take their game to the next level. To empathize (an important skill to enjoy life with a golfer), imagine the warmth and excitement you feel when you find that 30% off coupon for Target®.

Golf is a game in which the slowest people in the world are those in front of you, and the fastest are those behind.

Essential Equipment

Clubs

Clubs are the weapons a golfer uses in pursuit of a lower score. According to the rules of golf, a player is limited to carrying no more than fourteen (14) clubs at one time in his or her bag.

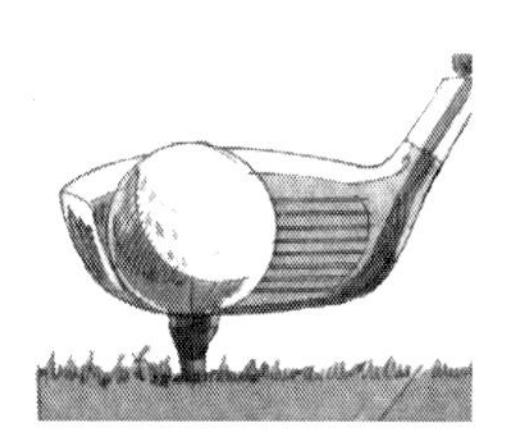

- Woods are the longest clubs and normally hit the ball the farthest. In a typical bag, you will find a driver and two or three fairway woods. The most common woods are a 3-wood and 5-wood. Women and seniors may also add a 7-wood or 9-wood for better control and distance. Prior to 1979, the heads of these clubs were made of persimmon wood. That was the year that TaylorMade®, a major golf equipment producer, introduced "metal woods." Persimmon was replaced by either steel or titanium alloy. Clubs made of wood have been relegated to antique stores and museums (or to kids like me who didn't know any better).
- Drivers are used to hit golf balls off the tee (the first shot taken on a hole).
- Fairway Woods are used to strike the ball from the ground when the green is a long distance away (usually the second or third shot on a hole). On occasion, you may hear the jubilation of a player who has successfully hit the green with such a shot.

- Rescue clubs combine elements of a wood and an iron. Made of metal, they are supposedly easier for the casual golfer to use than a fairway wood.
- Irons are the clubs most likely to be used from the fairway, although they are often hit from the tee, especially on par-3 holes. Irons feature thin, grooved faces of varying lofts. They are designated by number, the most common selection of irons being 3-iron through pitching wedge. The lower the number the lower trajectory and greater distance expected. I know. A higher number should designate more power, but remember that golf is a is a game of paradoxes: the winner in golf is the one with the lower score.
- Wedges are highly lofted irons often used to hit the ball from bunkers or in any situation when a high ball trajectory is desired. Some golfers carry as many as three wedges at a time. This is in case they happen to fling an uncooperative club into a nearby pond.
- Putters are used to roll the ball on the green. Players may own several putters but normally carry just one in their bag. This is why you will rarely see a golfer break his putter over his knee in the same way that he might a wedge.

Balls

Under the Rules of Golf, a golf ball can weigh no more than 1.62 oz. (45.93 grams), have a diameter not less than 1.68 in. (42.67 mm.), and much perform within specified velocity, distance, and symmetry limits. Golf balls are tested by the Royal and Ancient Golf Club of St Andrews and the United States Golf Association.

Those that do not conform to regulations may not be used in competitions.

A perfectly smooth golf ball with no dimples would travel less than 150 yards off the tee. A similarly hit ball with well-designed dimples will travel over 300 yards. Dimples are indentations on the surface that provide for more aerodynamic ball flight. Most golf balls have between 250 and 450 dimples.

Billions of golf balls have been manufactured. This is because the inevitable fate of golf balls is to get lost, cut, or to become otherwise unplayable. Most golf balls presently lie at the bottom of lakes or are carried off by ground hogs to their dens (an explanation used when a golfer loses a ball in the middle of a fairway.) Some wayward balls are recovered and resold as used or "experienced" balls.

Used balls may cost as low as $5.00 a dozen while twelve new top of the line balls cost $50.00 or more. Advertisers work hard to convince us that the more expensive a ball is the better it will play. The fact is, for 99% of golfers, if a ball has not been cut or turned into an ellipsoid, it will probably play as well as any.

Every golf ball carries a manufacturer's logo and a number. The number serves only to help a player identify his ball among the many others flying around the course. Some golfers put personalized marks on their balls. Professional golfer Duffy Waldorf lets his children scribble on his before tournaments.

In the second James Bond film, 007 turned the tables on his cheating nemesis Auric Goldfinger by swapping his ball with that of a different number when he wasn't looking. His opponent continued to play with the different ball and was later disqualified.

Regarding colors, there is no rule governing the color of the golf ball. Different colors are used to increase visibility or to express the golfer's personality. Balls are predominately white, though yellow, orange, and pink are also popular.

Bags

Early golf bags were 4½ inches wide and 35 inches tall, made of plain canvas and leather, with a metal disk at the bottom. Today's golf bags are spacious things made of high-tech plastics, polymers, metal compounds, leathers, and even furs. Most are adorned with various logos and such. Pockets and compartments accommodate cell phones, cameras, and sport drinks. Golf bags have hand straps and shoulder straps for carrying, and sometimes have retractable legs that allow it to stand upright when at rest. Bags are often pulled on two or three-wheeled carts or harnessed to a motorized cart.

Non-Essential Equipment

Gloves

Many golfers wear a golf glove. Interestingly, a right-handed player wears the glove on the left hand and vice versa. Gloves are made of leather (most expensive) and synthetic leather (least expensive). Gloves help keep a secure grip on the club during a swing. Gloves used to be worn at all times during a round. In the 1960s, when Arnold Palmer began to dominate the professional tour, he routinely removed his glove when preparing to putt. As a result, most golfers now remove the glove before putting.

Shoes

Golf shoes resemble everyday shoes except for metal or plastic spikes that protrude from the soles. This is to increase traction and help the player keep his/her balance during the swing. Professional players still use metal spikes, but in the mid-1990s golf courses began requiring golfers to use only "soft" plastic spikes in order to reduce damage to the course, especially on the greens. However, this hasn't translated into reduced fees due to lower maintenance costs.

Carts

Carts come in two models – pulled and motorized. Many golfers own carts that they pull behind them as they walk around a course. Few golfers can afford to own motorized carts that are driven with the bags harnessed at the rear – with the exception of retired doctors and lawyers in the Sun Belt. Most golf courses provide motorized carts for a rental fee.

Club Covers

These are fabric or plastic covers slipped over the heads of clubs to protect them from unnecessary wear. They are often decorative and expressive of a player's personality.

Chapter 4

Golf Etiquette – or Will Someone Explain that Weird Thing She Just Did?

Every family has a code of behavior. Most of these are unwritten yet clearly understood.

- Keep your elbows off the table.
- Keep your hands off each other
- Don't disturb Dad when he is in the recliner, especially when he is asleep and drooling.

Some find it difficult to understand how these serve to preserve important family values. Parents say that it is all for the good of the kids. The kids disagree and when they grow up spend large fees for therapy.

Golf has a rulebook of 164 pages. Breaking a rule can get you disqualified in a match. But going against golf's unwritten etiquette can get you bad looks at best and, at worst, relegation to a life of playing as a single.

A quote from the official USGA website:

"Unlike many sports, golf is played, for the most part, without the supervision of a referee or umpire. The game relies on the integrity of the individual to show consideration for other players and to abide by the Rules. All players should conduct themselves in a disciplined manner, demonstrating courtesy and sportsmanship at all times, irrespective of how competitive they may be. This is the spirit of the game of golf."[4]

Golf etiquette falls into four categories.

1. Player Safety

Since golfers often escape to golf courses from otherwise emotionally, physically, or maritally dangerous lives, their fellow players should never place them in harm's way. In such a spirit,

[4] www.USGA.org

- Never swing your club in a manner that might strike another.
- Never strike your ball until those ahead of you are out of range.
- If you hit a ball and it flies toward another player, you should immediately shout a warning. "Duck!" or "Hey you!" are not helpful. The universal term is "fore!"

2. Consideration for Other Players

While golf tends to be a solitary sport, it is never experienced alone. Like life, one's behavior has a direct or indirect impact on everyone else for good or ill.

- Pretend you are in the library. Do not disturb the play of others by moving, talking, or making any unnecessary noise (i.e., "Turn off that cell phone or I will hit it off the next tee!")
- At the tee box, wait until it is your turn to play before teeing the ball. (i.e., "How do you expect me to concentrate on my ball when yours is sitting there looking at me!")
- Keep your voice down, except for the rare occasions when you hole a put longer than twenty feet or hold a green with any club longer than a six iron.
- Do not stand directly behind the ball or directly behind the hole when someone else is about to play. On the green, note each player's putting line and avoid stepping into it. When he is making a stroke, do not cast a shadow upon it. (i.e., "If I want obstacles in my, way I'd play miniature golf.")
- When marking your ball, if the marker would be in the line of another player, move it a club head length to the side.

When it's your turn to putt, place the ball on the ground in front of your marker then remove the marker.

- Sometimes you can offer another player to "tend the pin." This is standing arm's length from the hole and holding the flagstick while another player putts. The flagstick must be pulled out before the ball reaches the hole or the putter will suffer a penalty under the Rules of Golf.
- Stay on or close to the green until the other players in your group have finished. (i.e., "If I have to watch you putt, you have to watch me too!")

3. Pace of Play

- Arrive at the golf course at least twenty minutes before your scheduled tee (start) time.
- One practice swing is enough.
- Keep up with those who are playing ahead of you. If you are delayed, (e.g., looking for a lost ball), you should invite those coming along behind you to play through
- You should be ready to play as soon as it is your turn to play (i.e., Play "ready golf").
- On the first hole, the player with the lowest handicap tees off first. From there, the person whose ball is farthest from the green plays next.
- The player with the best score on the previous hole has the honor of teeing off first on the next hole. If there is no outright winner of a hole, then the order of play does not change from the previous tee. In informal games one can

play ready golf and not wait for the best score on the hole to tee it up first.

- Pick up your tee after hitting your drive. If you break your tee, throw the pieces into a waste can or into the weeds. Do not leave the pieces scattered on the tee.
- You should not run during play, but instead walk quickly and remain stationary while others play their shots.
- Decide which club to use before you get to your ball.
- If you believe you may have hit your ball into a water hazard or out of bounds, you should play a provisional shot before looking for your ball.
- When going to the green, you should leave your bag or cart where you can quickly move to the next tee when finished.
- The player whose ball is farthest from the hole plays first. If the shot is not made, then the ball can be marked while others play their shots. The ball can be "tapped in" if it is within a foot of the hole.
- Head covers look impressive on the first tee, but need not be replaced thereafter.

4. Care of the Course

Bunkers

- Always enter a bunker from the low side or along the easiest slope.
- After playing a shot from a bunker, use a rake (usually found alongside the bunker) to carefully smooth over all divots and footprints you have made.

- Never pull carts into or lay bags down in bunkers.

Greens

- You should carefully repair all damage to the putting green made by the impact of a ball (whether or not made by the player himself). Tamp down all spike marks with the bottom of a putter.
- To avoid damaging the hole, do not step within a one-foot radius of the hole. Take care during the handling of the flagstick and the removal of a ball from the hole to not damage the hole. Do not use the head of a club to remove a ball from the hole.

Fairways

- Repair all divots, either by placing sand in the divot or replacing the grass.
- Park golf carts on the cart path when at the tee box or putting green. Carts should normally stay only on the paths, and are required to do so on many courses.
- When driving carts off established paths, observe the "90 degree rule": make a 90 degree turn off the path toward the fairway to a given ball, and return straight back to the path, not along the path of greatest convenience. Always set the park brake when leaving the cart.

A Word about Clothing

> Staff: Brookville Golf Course, may I help you?
> *Caller*: Do you have a dress code?
> Staff: Yes, we do. We require soft spikes.
> *Caller*: How about clothes?
> Staff: Yes, you have to wear clothes.

There was a time when a man who was summoned to the courthouse who didn't own a dress shirt or tie, would beg his friends and relatives for one. He wouldn't dare show up casually before the judge. Likewise, women left their sweatshirts and cutoffs in the drawer and reached deeper into their closets for their Sunday dresses.

Golf courses remain the few places in modern society with dress codes. The thought is that dressing appropriately shows respect for the friend who invited you, the other members of your group, and for the ancient game of golf.

- Shirts must have collars.
- Denim is never appropriate.
- Shorts must be designed for golf (i.e., not gym shorts or cutoffs). For men they should be no shorter than just above

the knee. Light colored socks go with white or saddle style shoes; black socks with black shoes.

- Long pants should have no cuffs since they trap dirt. Socks should match your trousers.
- Golf clothes are often bright and colorful, but not all at the same time! A classic combination of brown or blue with khaki is a good start.
- Wear street shoes to the course and change into your golf shoes in the locker room, not at your car in the parking lot.
- Hats help keep the sun off your face, and may improve your vision. Either baseball style or straw golf hats are appropriate.
- In cooler weather or early tee times, a golf sweater, vest, or jacket is practical.

Chapter 5

The Lofty World of the Golfing Gods (i.e., Professional Golfers)

95% of people who make a living in golf are not touring professionals. These are the men and women who staff golf pro shops, teach lessons, and oversee the thousands of golf courses across the country.

Less than five thousand (5,000) human beings at any one time play golf "on tour." Here are some recent numbers:

- PGA Tour golfers (230)
- Champions Tour golfers – for players 50 and over (369)
- Nationwide Tour golfers - think AAA baseball (318)
- Mini-Tour golfers - think single A baseball (less than 600)

The above total includes female professionals and those who tour in Europe and Asia. For every "touring pro" there are 5,600 "golfing Joes" around America who wish they had the time, talent, or luck to live the dream at some level.

The closest most can get is through a video game system such as Nintendo Wii® or Xbox Kinect® that allows virtual play on courses around the world in the persona of a golf professional. There is no feeling like sinking a virtual birdie putt on the virtual "road hole" at a virtual St. Andrews to beat virtual Tiger

Woods (or Jack Nicklaus if you're from an earlier generation) for The Open Championship.

Another way to approach the world of the golf gods is to show up "outside the ropes" as a spectator at a professional tournament. Last Christmas, I talked my wife into letting me buy tickets for a PGA event coming to my town later this year. It was a great deal so she agreed. I'm happy!

Golf is a sport that can be played competitively at all ages. You can play golf even with one, two, three or four artificial limbs. The dream never has to die in golf like it does in football, baseball, or basketball.

I will never forget being in my early forties and following a group of my golf heroes for eighteen holes at a Champions event: Arnold Palmer, Gary Player, and Lee Trevino. I remembering listening to their conversation. Some of the bolder members of gallery even got into conversations with them between shots. They hit many shots that day, and I remember watching amazed as one after the other they each drove the green of the 311 yard Hole 14 at the Brickyard Crossing Course in Indianapolis. Yes Virginia, there is a Santa Claus.

Fantasy Golf is a growing pastime. This is a where golfing Joe can imagine running his own team of professional golfers via the Internet. Play coincides with the PGA Tour season. At the beginning of the season, you choose an eight-man team from among three groupings of golfers of various abilities. Before each tournament, the fantasy golfer selects a starting foursome. Reserves can be brought in between rounds to take the place of struggling starters. The challenge is not only to pick the best team week in and week out, but also to manage the team in a way that produces the best possible fantasy score.

On Tour

Q-School

This is short for "qualifying school." The PGA Tour offers this qualifying tournament once a year to determine who will have the right to play in PGA events the next twelve months. Q-School is mandatory for nearly all tour professionals, especially those who did not complete the previous season in the top 125 places in monetary winnings. Years ago, there was a formal educational aspect to it, but nowadays it is a straight-forward and often emotionally brutal competition. Only the top twenty-five plus ties of 160 players who start the six-round event receive their "cards." The next fifty finishers can still play golf professionally on the Nationwide Tour.

The Champions and European Tours conduct their own Q-schools.

Tournaments

The professional golf season begins in Hawaii in January before moving to the West Coast and then to Florida in March. As weather in the US warms, competitions head north.

Most tournaments are four 18-hole rounds conducted over consecutive days (Thursday - Sunday). Champions Tour events consist of 54 holes (Friday - Sunday). The lowest number of strokes taken wins. Fields are cut after 36 holes (except on the Champions Tour) to the low 70 scores plus ties. Only those golfers who "make the cut" will go home with any money. The cut rules are different in Major tournaments. For instance, in the U.S. Open all golfers in the top 60 plus ties, and any golfer within 10 strokes of the lead, make the cut.

The Fed Ex® Cup

This is a season-long competition in which golfers earn points based upon their performance in tournaments. Some events award more points than others based on the perceived difficulty of field. The season concludes with four tournaments that reduce the field to thirty players. These finalists then vie for the title and a ten million dollar prize.

Majors

Four tournament titles are the most sought after and attract the best golfers in the world.

- The Masters (April)
- The U.S. Open (June)
- The British Open (July)

- The PGA Championship (August)

> Tiger Woods is the only golfer in history to win every major within a twelve-month period, although not in the same calendar year (2000-2001)

World Rankings

All professional golfers are ranked against each other. A list of the top one thousand golfers is maintained by Official World Golf Ranking® (a precise if unimpressive name). The formula used is both complicated and controversial, but until something better comes along, it is endorsed by all the professional golf tours. As of this writing, an Englishman is the top golfer while a golfer from India is number 1000.

International Tournaments

The Ryder Cup

This biannual match play competition is between male golfers of the United States and Europe. Over three days, teams of twelve golfers play in a variety of formats including foursomes (alternate shot), four-ball, and singles. Winning teams or players are awarded one point for their side. Matches that tie earn ½ point for each side. The first team to earn 14½ points wins the tournament. The venue alternates between courses in each part of the world. No prize money is awarded to the winners.

The President's Cup

This biannual series of men's golf matches is between teams representing the United States and all other nations minus

Europe. The format is the same as the Ryder Cup and no prize money is awarded to the winners.

The Solheim Cup

This biannual competition began in 1990. It pits an International team of women golfers against those from the United States.

Quotes from some Golfing Greats:

The greens were so fast, I had to hold my putter over the ball and hit it with the shadow.
—Sam Snead

The first time I played the Masters, I was so nervous I drank a bottle of rum before I teed off. I shot the happiest 83 of my life.
—Chi Chi Rodriguez

You've just got one problem. You stand too close to the ball after you've hit it.
—Sam Snead to a Duffer

I don't enjoy playing video golf because there is nothing to throw.
—Paul Azinger

I've broken or thrown a few clubs in my day. I guess at one time or another, I probably held distance records for every club in the bag.
—Tommy Bolt

My swing is so bad that I look like a caveman killing his lunch.
—Lee Trevino

The golf swing is like sex. You can't be thinking of the mechanics of the act while you are performing.
—Dave Hill

I lost a ball in the rough today. I dropped another ball over my shoulder and lost it too. And while looking for that one, I lost my caddie.
—Jock Hutchinson on the 1926 US Open course conditions

Chapter 6

Match Play, Scrambles, and Other Variations on the Game

The standard approach to golf is "stroke or medal play." This is when players add up the total amount of drives, fairway shots, approach shots, chips, pitches, putts, and penalty strokes taken to move the golf ball from the tee to the green over eighteen holes.

Another way to play golf is "match play." This is played and scored on a per hole basis. The player/team scoring lowest on a hole wins that hole. If the players/teams tie than neither wins the hole and play continues to the next hole. To be "up" a hole or holes is to be leading. To be "down" a hole or holes is to be losing.

Too many focus on lowering their handicaps in hopes of becoming a scratch golfer. Golf is a game that allows players to be as creative as they want to be, as long as everyone is in agreement at the first tee. For instance,

Gruesomes

Both members of Team A tee off. Then the members of the opposing side select which drive Team A has to play (obviously the worse or more gruesome of the two). When Team B's golfers tee off, Team A returns the favor. Following tee shots, the teams play out the hole in alternate shot fashion, except that the player who hit the gruesome tee ball also plays the second shot for his or her side.

Whack and Hack

Four team members each play their own ball for four individual scores. Two of those scores are combined to make up the team score on each hole. The two scores that are used are the low ball and the high ball. So if the four players score 4, 5, 6 and 7, respectively, the team score is 11 (4 + 7). There is one exception: if the low score for the team is a birdie or better, then the team gets to use its two low scores on that hole.

Pink Lady

One golfer in a four-person team plays a pink golf ball. The golfers tee off and play a scramble (see below), and on each hole two of the golfers' scores are combined for the team score. One of those is the low score among the three golfers using their regular golf balls; and the other is the score of the golfer using the pink ball. The golfer with the pink ball—the Pink Lady—is under a lot of pressure to come through for the team. On each hole, that ball rotates among the four players in the group.

Fish

This is a betting game for groups of golfers modeled after a popular fishing bet, hence its name. The fishing bet is threefold: who catches the first fish, the biggest fish, and the most fish. Fish on a golf course involves birdies: who makes the first birdie, the longest birdie, and the most birdies. Each of the three bets carries its own dollar amount.

Bag Raid

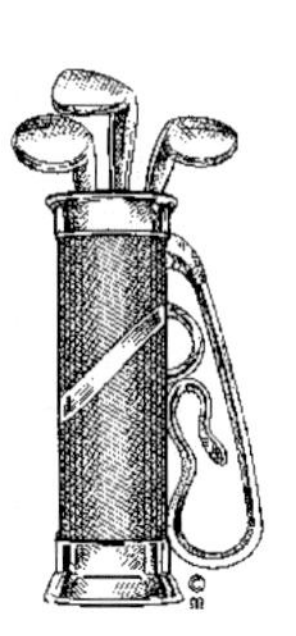

This is a match play game between two golfers. Each time one wins a hole, his opponent gets to remove a club from the winner's bag. Example: After A wins the first hole, B removes A's pitching wedge from play. For the rest of the round, A cannot use that pitching wedge. Bag Raid is usually played with the putter having immunity.

Bingo Bango Bongo

This points-based game can be played by any number of players. Three types of achievements are rewarded with a point. The first player in a group to get his ball on the green gets a point (bingo). The player in the group whose ball is closest to the pin once all balls are on the green gets a point (bango). And the player in the group who is first to hole out gets a point (bongo). Add up the points at the end of the game. High points wins.

Chicago

Golfers beginning their rounds with negative points based on handicaps. Points are added during the round to get from the negative to the positive, clearing your "hurdle" (the term used for your starting total of negative points) by as much as possible. Negative points begin at -39 for scratch golfers. A 1-handicapper starts with -38, a 2-handicapper with -37, and so on up to a 36-

handicapper who starts with -3 points. Bogeys earn l point, pars 2 points, birdies 4 points, and eagles 8 points. The highest point total—whether that is 15 or minus-15—wins.

Shoot Out

A field of 19 players begins the round. On each hole, one player is eliminated until only one remains—the champion, crowned on the 18th hole. This is a slow game, especially in the early going, because all remaining players must complete each hole before play moves on. On each hole, the high score is eliminated. Ties can be broken through playoffs using skill challenges such as holing a putt from a set distance or closest chip to the hole.

Tombstone

Golfers begin their rounds with an allotment of strokes and they play until their strokes run out. The golfer who makes it farthest around the golf course is the winner. The name comes from the fact that each golfer carries with him a flag, a small clipboard or other item to be staked in the ground at the point of their final stroke. The tombstone is the object placed in the ground where the golfer's round meets its end.

Nassau

Many golfers enjoy making friendly wagers on the course. A Nassau is one of the most popular golfing bets. It's essentially three wagers in one: lowest score on the front nine, the back nine, and total 18-hole scores. As a bet, the most common form is the $2 Nassau. The front nine is worth $2, the back nine is worth

$2 and the 18-hole total is worth $2. A player or team sweeping all three wins $6.

Skins

Each hole represents a skin and in order to 'win' that skin a golfer must score better than all the other competitors on that hole. If no one wins, the skin is carried over to the next hole. At the end of 18 holes the total number of strokes does not matter. The winner is determined by the player with the most skins.

Best Ball

Each player on a team plays his/her own ball for the entire round, and the team records the individual score from the low team member on each hole. The best scores are then totaled for the team's final 18 hole score.

Scramble

All players in a group hit a shot from the tee, then choose the best shot and each hit from that spot until the ball is holed.

Four-Ball

Two person teams compete in a foursome against each other using the best individual score from each team as the team score on each hole.

Stableford

Players earn points based on their score in relation to par. Par earns no points. Birdies earn 2 points. Eagles earn 5 points. Double eagles earn 8 points. On the other hand, bogies lose 1 point and double bogeys or worse lose 3 points. The winner is the player with the highest number of points.

Alternate Shot

Two golfers play as a team and take turns hitting the same golf ball. They decide among themselves who tees off on the first hole. Player A hits the opening tee ball. They walk to the ball and Player B hits the second shot. Player B takes the third stroke and Player B the fourth. This continues until the ball is in the hole. On the next hole Player B hits the tee shot.

Chapter 7

Playing a Round

A golf course can seem like alien territory to someone who plays only occasionally. An example of this might be an employee who supervisor has asked him to join a foursome from his company to play in a benefit scramble. Scramble? What's that mean? Or maybe your husband's country club is raising funds with a golf marathon for husband and wife teams. Does that mean you have to run from hole to hole? The answer could be as important as finding out that your new girlfriend really likes golf.

Is there a way to play eighteen holes of golf with minimum embarrassment and maximum enjoyment? The answer is **yes** and that's what this last chapter is about.

Attitude

Playing satisfying golf starts with the proper attitude. Too many players see golf as a problem to be solved rather than a pastime to enjoy. One of the most well-known books on the game is called *Golf is Not a Game of Perfect,* written Dr. Bob Rotella. Professional golfer Brad Faxon provided this testimony: "I was at a point where I was taking golf so seriously that I wasn't enjoying it any more. [This book] taught me to throw away doubt and fear, and as a result I am enjoying golf, learning more, and playing better."

Most problems on the golf course happen when golfers measure themselves against perfect (i.e. par). While it may help to visualize the intended flight path of the ball before swinging, too much intensity can shrink a very wide fairway into a narrow ribbon. It may be enough for the casual golfer that the ball got from the tee to the cup. When I get stressed over a couple of bad shots, I tell myself, "I've paid too much money to come here and just be miserable." Other times I grade my performance in a round not in terms of strokes under par, but rather in whether I left the course with more balls in my bag than when I started!

Whether one is a new player or tour pro, the best way to approach the game is with a paradoxical blend of focus and nonchalance. Golf is a sport in which scores are recorded, but most of all it is an experience that should be determined by more than the sum of the stroke on a hole or in a round. No matter what happened the last time, every swing is a new opportunity. Every hole is a new beginning. Every course is a new adventure.

This chapter is not so much about playing better golf. It's really about enjoying a shared experience. Most healthy golf is played in the company of others and most golfers can tell stories of people they played with and never will again. Jack Nicklaus tells about when he was a teenager and he and his father would play golf. The younger Nicklaus would often lose his temper over a bad shot. On one occasion he threw an iron down the fairway. His father told him that the next time he did that they would never play together again. It got through to him and he went on to become the greatest golfer of all time. Years later he would say, "Ask yourself how many shots you would have saved if you never lost your temper, never got down on yourself, always developed a strategy before you hit, and always played within your own capabilities."

Many friendships that start during a round of golf endure through the years. Whether or not you play three times a week or just twice a year, there is every reason to expect golf to be a game that stays an enjoyable part of your life for a long time.

Another quote from Jack Nicklaus: "I'm a firm believer in the theory that people only do their best at things they truly enjoy. It is difficult to excel at something you don't enjoy."

At the Course

Congratulations! You have accepted an invitation to play a round with a friend or loved one. Dress appropriately for the weather and the course's dress code and plan to arrive at the course thirty minutes ahead of your scheduled tee time. If the *greens fees* weren't paid for in advance, you will check in, perhaps at the *pro shop*. Most corporate outings provide motorized carts used by a pair of golfers to move around the course. Your more experienced partner will likely drive the cart to your car where you can load your golf bags into the cart's rear compartment and then secure them with the straps provided. If it is just a friendly round you have the option of walking – either carrying your bags or pulling them on two-wheeled carts - or renting a motorized cart.

You can play golf in standard athletic shoes, but if you have spiked golf shoes (soft spikes are required at nearly all courses these days) you can wear them inside the course's buildings (i.e. pro shop, snack bar, bathrooms, locker rooms) as long as you clean dirt and loose grass from them using the brush/scrapers provided.

If you don't own your own set of clubs, golf courses normally provide a set for a reasonable rental fee. Most beginners can get by with a driver, a five, seven, and nine iron, a wedge, and a putter. A full set of clubs includes eight more woods and irons. Take plenty of tees (at least eighteen) and golf balls. Having a ball repair tool is good form.

Starting the Round

Many outings start golfers at the same time at different holes. This is what is called a *shotgun start*. For instance, you may start on hole number five and will finish the round on hole number four.

Tees are arranged with different colored markers designating starting points for men, women, and seniors. You are allowed to tee your ball within a space defined as between the markers, no more than two club lengths behind the markers, and no closer to the green than a line drawn between the markers. Some golfers decide who goes first by flipping a tee in the air. When it lands on the ground, the player standing most in the path of the tee's point goes first.

A general practice is to hit a tee shot with a *driver* (#1 wood) if the hole is a par four or par five. An *iron* is typically used on par threes. This is all subjective, based upon the distance the player knows he can drive the ball. In addition, many new players leave the driver in the bag because they find they are able to *keep the ball in play* better by using irons on all tee shots.

Let's say the aforementioned tossed tee pointed your way. You pull your driver from your bag and place the ball on the tee. After taking a maximum of two practice swings, you drive the ball a very respectable (for an inexperienced golfer) 175 yards down the fairway. Now what? As your playing companions take their turns you should stand still in a place that allows them to see you but not be distracted by you. Follow the flight of the ball and spot its possible location using helpful landmarks (i.e. trees, stakes, etc.). Just like it takes a village to raise a child, it often takes the whole foursome to locate one player's ball.

Through the Green

If you are playing a team scramble, everyone will take his next shot from where the best - usually the longest - drive landed. This procedure is followed for the rest of the round and the team's score is posted at the end. Individual scores are not kept. Scrambles are a very attractive form of golf for those who don't play very often. This is because since there are four chances to hit a good shot every time, the pressure is much less – unless the three previous shots were poor and it is up to the fourth to pull off a winner!

What if you are playing your own ball? Let's go back to your drive of 175 yards. The player who is farthest from the green takes the next turn to hit – probably you. An exception to this is when everyone has agreed to play *ready golf*. This means that you hit your ball whenever you are ready, assuming that no one is in your line of fire.

There are basic things that golfers of every skill level need to do in order to hit the ball as far and as straight as each circumstance requires.

Take a Proper Grip

New golfers usually grip the club in the same way as baseball players grip a bat: a two-fisted grip with the hands pressed tightly together. While this works in baseball, it inhibits proper action through the golf swing. It also reduces the feel that is so important in fine-tuning your swing as you mature as a player.

For a right-handed golfer, the left hand grips the club near the butt end of the shaft while the right hand is placed next on the shaft nearer to the clubhead. The opposite is true for lefties.

There are two variations on the golf grip. Some golfers overlap the forefinger of the left hand over the pinky finger of the right. Others interlock these two fingers. Many golfers extend the right thumb along the golf shaft, while others curl it over slightly. A further adaptation is what's called a weak or strong grip. This does not mean one grip is better than the other. More advanced golfers rotate their hands clockwise or counterclockwise around the shaft in order to produce either a *draw* or a *fade*. The best goal for beginners is to keep the ball in play by routinely hitting it straight.

The good news is that whatever peculiarities a golfer settles on, the golf grip remains basically the same for drives, fairway shots, chips and putts.

Line up with the Target

This is what is called the *set up*. The target may be the green (on par 3s), two hundred yards out in the middle of the fairway, or anywhere except the stream that sits between you and a safe landing.

There are many body parts that have to function as one to hit a successful golf shot. At the setup, the three most important are the shoulders, the hips, and the toes. Draw an imaginary line through all three and make sure all point at your target. Even though a lot of problems can happen during the swing, it is much more likely that the ball will travel in the direction you intend if these three line up. If it is hard for you to tell how you are lined up, be humble enough to ask an honest and compassionate friend for her perspective.

Contact the Ball Cleanly at the Bottom of the Swing

As I said, this is where most of the learning happens. No one starts out driving the golf ball 300 yards or dripping pitch shots within three feet of the pin. Because this is a simple guide, I won't delve into all the bodily mechanics of the golf swing. If thinking of your arms and the club as a pendulum helps then do so. The point is making solid contact with the ball. There is no one perfect swing (just watch Arnold Palmer in his prime or Jim Furyk today!)

One good piece of advice is that nearly every golfer has to find a way to resist the temptation to not keep his head down through the swing. Even experienced golfers need to do this. A pro once taught me about driving the golf ball: "Make sure you can see the grass beneath the ball after it leaves the tee." It works. This somehow keeps the body in a better position to strike the ball.

Finally, the key to hitting the ball straight is to swing level and make sure the face of the club is square to the ball. During the swing the clubhead needs to be following a circular route that does not push or pull the ball off line. This will take lots of practice and awareness of one's body movements. At the same time, the clubface should not be turned to the right or left when impacting the ball. This will also take practice. Perhaps you are coming to understand that golf is a game of incremental changes that result either in great despair or great joy.

A Word About Putting

There's an ancient piece of golf advice that dates back to the early Scottish hearty men who braved the icy winds off the North Sea in order to challenge each other to a match: "Drive for show, but putt for dough." In other words, any *ox* can drive a golf ball out of sight; it takes real skill to consistently roll a putt longer than four feet and sink it to win the bet or purse.

Putting is all about feel.

- Nothing in your body should be moving except your shoulders (think the pendulum of a clock).
- Keep your wrists firm (do not flick them).
- Fix your eyes on the ball (do not raise them to follow its course).
- Take the club back on a straight line approximately an inch for every foot the ball needs to travel.
- Accelerate through the ball approximately the same distance as your backswing, moving the club on the same straight line.
- Strike the ball in the middle of the clubface.
- Make sure the putter is moving parallel with the ground at impact (not descending or ascending).

All teaching pros and instruction books focus on variations on these mechanics. The point here is that the prospect of hitting a golf ball a respectable way down a fairway does not have to be intimidating. As Jack Nicklaus said, play within your capabilities. Even he had to learn how to hit the ball straight before he hit it far. He just learned it more quickly than 99.9% of the rest of humanity.

In Trouble

The fundamental spirit and rule of golf is to play one's ball *where it lies*. This means that it is illegal and bad form to improve the situation in which you find your ball. In other words, don't touch or move your ball in any way.

One exception to the above commandment is on the putting green. There it is permissible to mark the spot of your ball with a coin, pick up the ball in order to clean it, and then replace it in its original position.

What if you hit your ball into a creek, pond or other body of water? You are allowed to retrieve your ball if the water is not too deep. Experienced golfers carry a ball retriever in their bag that allows them to reach into hazards and pick up balls without getting themselves wet. This ball can then be played - with a penalty stroke added to the score.

If your ball ends up somewhere that you cannot swing at it - under a bush, between some rocks, up in a tree - you must take an unplayable lie, place the ball in an open space no closer to the hole, and then play on. Remember to add that dratted penalty stroke to your score. Now do you see why scramble golf is so attractive?

Some hazards – like sand traps or bunkers – can be played out of without penalty. There are some special considerations here. First, you cannot touch the ground with your club in a bunker before you swing at the ball. Second, after your shot you must use a rake to smooth out the divot you made in the sand, along with your footprints.

If you hit your ball out of bounds in a scramble, it's no big deal. Your team has others yet to hit. If you are playing your own ball, you lose the distance, take a penalty stroke, and hit another ball from the same place as your original shot. For instance, your original shot was your second on that hole. It goes out of bounds. You place another ball in front of you and hit what is now your fourth shot. If you are not sure that the ball went out of bounds or is lost, you hit a provisional ball just in case. If you find your original ball, you pick up the provisional with no harm done.

On the Green

Eventually your ball will wind up on the green. Maybe you will launch a pretty lofted shot that lands softly. Chances on you will become well acquainted with what is called a chip shot. This kind of shot is taken from just off the green with an iron. The intent is to fly the ball over the thicker grass and land it on the green in a way that the ball rolls toward the cup and stops nearby - or hopefully goes in! Most golf shots are taken within fifty yards of the green. This means that this can become the most satisfying part of the game for everyone, yet so few golfers spend time practicing these shots. If you become good around the green, you'll be a popular person at the course!

One way to get some good practice on your short game is to spend time at a Par-3 course. This is a course composed of all Par-3 holes. Every tee shot has a chance to land on the green. Every shot is one that will help you get feel around the green. It will pay off in a big way.

Greens are special places and for this reason golfers take special care of them. They never pull or drive carts onto a green. Most courses require golf carts to be parked several yards away. Golfers also repair all marks they make to the green, whether indentations made by their balls or scrapes made by their spikes.

The golfer whose ball is closest to the hole normally removes the flagstick from the cup so that the others can putt. The flagstick can be laid down on the green out of the way. Golfers take turns, starting with the player whose ball is farthest from the hole. A special club called a putter is used for this. The putter has a flat surface with no loft and when swung correctly will roll the ball smoothly toward the hole.

Since there are other players on the course, it is always appropriate to leave the green as soon as the last player has finished. The first player to finish the hole is normally the one who retrieves the flagstick and places it back in the cup.

The first person to tee off on the next hole is the person who just shot the lowest score.

Finishing a Round

Over the roughly four hours it takes to play eighteen holes of golf there are many opportunities to encourage and commiserate with each other. Golf is a game of ups and downs. Some golfers welcome observations on their swings and others do not. Some like to talk about anything and everything. For others, it depends upon how they are playing.

Hopefully you can look back on your golfing experience and say the following:

1. You took care of the golf course.

- You repaired divots and fixed ball marks
- You drove the golf cart on designated paths and stayed away from all greens
- You packed all trash out or put it in designated receptacles.

2. You respected the play of the other golfers on the course

- You warned them of errant shots by calling out "fore."
- You kept quiet when they took their shots.
- You assisted them in looking for lost balls.
- You applauded their good play, even if yours was less than stellar.

3. You remember at least one satisfying moment that will bring you back for another round.
4. Or better yet, you find a practice range, pay for a bucket of practice balls and a basic lesson, and become an even more

enjoyable playing partner. You don’t have to become a great golfer to enjoy golf for a lifetime, just someone who more often than not hits the ball where you want it to go!

5. You get hooked and want to spend $1,000 on a set of new clubs. **Hopefully not!** $150 is more like it from any of the popular chain or sporting goods stores.